Fantasy on "The Last Rose of Summer"

By

Felix Mendelssohn

For Solo Piano

(1827)

Op.15

British Library Cataloguing-in-Publication Data
A catalogue record for this book is available from
the British Library

Jakob Ludwig Felix Mendelssohn-Bartholdy

German composer, grandson of **Moses Mendelssohn**, was born in Hamburg on the 3rd of February 1809. In consequence of the troubles caused by the French occupation of Hamburg, Abraham Mendelssohn, his father, migrated in 1811 to Berlin, where his grandmother Fromet, then in the twenty-fifth year of her widowhood, received the whole family into her house, No. 7 Neue Promenade. Here Felix and his sister Fanny received their first instruction in music from their mother, under whose care they progressed so rapidly that their exceptional talent soon became apparent. Their next teacher was Madame Bigot, who, during the temporary residence of the family in Paris in 1816, gave them valuable instruction. On their return to Berlin they took lessons in thoroughbass and composition from Zelter, in pianoforte-playing from Ludwig Berger, and in violin-playing from Henning the care of their general education being entrusted to the father of the novelist Paul Heyse.

Felix first played in public on the 24th of October 1818, taking the pianoforte part in a trio by Woelfl. On the 11th of April 1819 he entered the Berlin Singakademie as an alto, and in the following year began to compose with extraordinary rapidity. His earliest dated work is a cantata, *In rührend feierlichen Tonen*, completed on the 13th of January 1820. During that year alone he produced nearly sixty movements, including songs, pianoforte sonatas, a trio for pianoforte, violin and violoncello, a sonata for violin and pianoforte, pieces for the organ, and even a little dramatic piece in three scenes. In 1821 he wrote five symphonies for stringed instruments, each in three movements; motets for four voices, an opera, in one act, called *Soldatenliebschaft*; another, called *Die beiden Pädagogen*; part of a third, called *Die wandernden Comödianten*; and an immense quantity of other music of different kinds, all showing the precocity of his genius. The original autograph copies of these early productions are preserved in the Berlin Library, where they form part of a collection which fills forty-four large volumes, all written with infinite neatness, and for the most part carefully dated — a sufficient proof that the methodical habits which distinguished his later life were formed in early childhood.

In 1821 Mendelssohn paid his first visit to Goethe, with whom he spent sixteen days at Weimar, in company with Zelter. From this year also dates his first acquaintance with Weber, who was then in Berlin superintending the production of *Der Freischütz*; and from the summer of 1822 his introduction, at Cassel, to another of the greatest of his contemporaries, Ludwig Spohr. During this year his pen was even more prolific, producing, among other works, an opera, in three acts, entitled *Die beiden Neffen, oder der Onkel aus Boston*, and a pianoforte concerto, which he played in public at a concert given by Frau Anna Milder.

It had long been a custom with the Mendelssohn family to give musical performances on alternate Sunday mornings in their dining-room, with a small orchestra, which Felix always conducted, even when he was not tall enough to be seen without standing upon a stool. For each of these occasions he produced some new work — playing the pianoforte pieces himself, or entrusting them to Fanny, while his sister Rebecka sang, and his brother Paul played the violoncello. In this way *Die beiden Neffen* was first privately performed, on the fifteenth anniversary of his birthday, the 3rd of February 1824. Between the 3rd and the 31st of March in this year he composed his fine symphony in C minor, now known as Op. 10, and soon afterwards the quartet in B minor, Op. 3, and the (posthumous) pianoforte sestet, Op. 110. In this year also began his lifelong friendship with Moscheles, who, when asked to receive him as a pupil, said, "If he wishes to take a hint from me, as to anything new to him, he can easily do so; but he stands in no need of lessons."

In 1825 Abraham Mendelssohn took Felix to Paris, where among other musicians then resident in the French capital he met the two most popular dramatic composers of the age, Rossini and Meyerbeer, and lived on terms of intimacy with Hummel, Kalkbrenner, Rode, Baillot, Herz, and many other artists of European celebrity. On this occasion also he made his first acquaintance with Cherubini, who, though he rarely praised any one, expressed a high opinion of his talent, and recommended him to write a *Kyrie*, for five voices, with full orchestral accompaniments, which he himself described as "exceeding in thickness" anything he had attempted. From letters written at this period we learn that Felix's estimate of the French school of music was far from flattering; but he formed some friendships in Paris, which were renewed on later occasions. He returned to Berlin with his father in May 1825, taking leave of his Parisian friends on the 19th of the month, and interrupting his journey at Weimar for the purpose of paying a second visit to Goethe, to whom he dedicated his quartet in B minor. On reaching home he must have worked with greater zeal than ever; for on the 10th of August in this same year he completed an opera, in two acts, called *Die Hochzeit des Camacho*, a work of considerable importance.

No ordinary boy could have escaped uninjured from the snares attendant upon such a life as that which Mendelssohn now lived. Notwithstanding his overwhelming passion for music, his general education had been so well cared for that he was able to hold his own, in the society of his seniors, with the grace of an accomplished man of the world. He was already recognized as a leading spirit by the artists with whom he associated, and these artists were men of acknowledged talent and position. The temptations to egoism by which he was surrounded would have rendered most clever students intolerable. But the natural amiability of his disposition, and the healthy influence of his happy home-life, counteracted all tendencies towards self-assertion.

Soon after his return from Paris, Abraham Mendelssohn removed from his mother's residence to No. 3 Leipziger Strasse, a roomy, old-fashioned house, containing an excellent music-room, and in the grounds adjoining a "Gartenhaus" capable of accommodating several hundred persons at the Sunday performances. In the autumn of the following year this "garden-house" witnessed a memorable private performance of the work by means of which the greatness of Mendelssohn's genius was first revealed to the outer world the overture to Shakespeare's *Midsummer Night's Dream*. The finished score of this famous composition is dated "Berlin, August 6, 1826" — its author was only seventeen and a half years old. Yet in no later work does he exhibit more originality of thought, more freshness of conception, or more perfect mastery over the details of technical construction, than in this delightful inspiration. The overture was first publicly performed at Stettin, in February 1827, under the direction of the young composer, who was at once accepted as the leader of a new and highly characteristic manifestation of the spirit of progress. Henceforth we must speak of him, not as a student, but as a mature and experienced artist.

Meanwhile *Camacho's Wedding* had been submitted to Spontini, with a view to its production at the opera. The libretto, founded upon an episode in the history of Don Quixote, was written by Klingemann, and Mendelssohn threw himself into the spirit of the romance with a keen perception of its peculiar humour. The work was put into rehearsal soon after the composer's return from Stettin, produced on the 29th of April 1827, and received with great apparent enthusiasm; but a cabal was formed against it, and it never reached a second performance. The critics abused it mercilessly; yet it exhibits merits of a very high order. The solemn passage for the trombones, which heralds the first appearance of the knight of La Mancha, is conceived in a spirit of reverent appreciation of the idea of Cervantes, which would have done honour to a composer of lifelong experience.

Mendelssohn was annoyed at this injustice, and some time elapsed before his mind recovered its usual bright tone; but he continued to work diligently. Among other serious undertakings, he formed a choir for the study of the choral works of Sebastian Bach, then unknown to the public; and, in spite of Zelter's opposition, he succeeded, in 1829, in inducing the Berlin Singakademie to give a public performance of the *Passion according to St Matthew*, under his direction, with a chorus of between three and four hundred voices. The scheme succeeded beyond his warmest hopes, and proved the means of restoring to the world great compositions which had never been heard since the death of Bach. But the obstructive party were offended; and at this period Mendelssohn was far from popular among the musicians of Berlin.

In April 1829 Mendelssohn paid his first visit to London. His reception was enthusiastic. He made his first appearance before an English audience at one of the Philharmonic Society's concerts — then held in the Argyll Rooms — on the 25th of May, conducting his symphony in C minor from the pianoforte, to which he was led by John Cramer. On the 30th he played Weber's *Concertstück*, from memory, a proceeding at that time extremely unusual. At a concert given by Drouet, on the 24th of June, he played Beethoven's pianoforte concerto in E flat, which had never before been heard in the country; and the overture to *A Midsummer Night's Dream* was also, for the first time, presented to a London audience. On returning home from the concert, Attwood, then organist of St Paul's Cathedral, left the score of the overture in a hackney coach, whereupon Mendelssohn wrote out another, from memory, without an error. At another concert he played, with Moscheles, his still unpublished concerto in E, for two pianofortes and orchestra. After the close of the London season he started with Klingemann on a tour through Scotland, where he was inspired with the first idea of his overture to *The Isles of Fingal*, returning to Berlin at the end of November. Except for an accident to his knee, which lamed him for some time, his visit was highly successful and laid the foundation of many friendships and prosperous negotiations.

The visit to England formed the first division of a great scheme of travel which his father wished him to extend to all the most important art centres in Europe. After refusing the offer of a professorship at Berlin, he started again, in May 1830, for Italy, pausing on his way at Weimar, where he spent a fortnight with Goethe, and reaching Rome, after many pleasant interruptions, on the 1st of November. No excitement prevented him from devoting a certain time every day to composition; but he lost no opportunity of studying either the countless treasures which form the chief glory of the great city or the manners and customs of modern Romans. He attended, with insatiable curiosity, the services in the Sistine Chapel; and his keen power of observation enabled him to throw much interesting light upon them. His letters on this subject, however, lose much of their value through his incapacity to comprehend the close relation existing between the music of Palestrina and his contemporaries and the ritual of the Roman Church. His Lutheran education kept him in ignorance even of the first principles of ordinary chanting; and it is amusing to find him describing as enormities peculiar to the papal choir customs familiar to every village singer in England, and as closely connected with the structure of the "Anglican chant" as with that of "Gregorian music." Still, though he could not agree in all points with Baini, the greatest ecclesiastical musician then living, he shared his admiration for the *Improperia*, the *Miserere*, and the *cantus planus* of the *Lamentationes* and the *Exultet*, the musical beauty of which he could understand, apart from their ritual significance.

In passing through Munich on his return in October 1831 he composed and played his pianoforte concerto in G minor, and accepted a commission (never fulfilled) to compose an opera for the Munich theatre. Pausing for a time at Stuttgart, Frankfort and Düsseldorf he arrived in Paris in December, and passed four pleasant months in the renewal of acquaintances formed in 1825, and in close intercourse with Liszt and Chopin. On the 19th of February 1832 the overture to *A Midsummer Night's Dream* was played at the conservatoire, and many of his other compositions were brought before the public; but he did not escape disappointments with regard to some of them, especially the Reformation symphony, and the visit was brought to a premature close in March by an attack of cholera, from which, however, he rapidly recovered.

On the 23rd of April 1832 he was again in London, where he twice played his G minor concerto at the Philharmonic concerts, gave a performance on the organ at St Paul's, and published his first book of *Lieder ohne Worte*. He returned to Berlin in July, and during the winter he gave public performances of his Reformation symphony, his concerto in G minor, and his *Walpurgisnacht*. In the following spring he paid a third visit to London for the purpose of conducting his Italian symphony, which was played for the first time, by the Philharmonic Society, on the 13th of May 1833. On the 26th of the same month he conducted the performances at the Lower Rhine festival at Düsseldorf with such brilliant effect that he was at once offered, and accepted, the appointment of general-music-director to the town, an office which included the management of the music in the principal churches, at the theatre, and at the rooms of two musical associations.

Before entering upon his new duties, Mendelssohn paid a fourth visit to London, with his father, returning to Düsseldorf on the 27th of September 1833. His influence produced an excellent effect upon the church music and in the concert-room; but his relations with the management of the theatre were not altogether pleasant; and it was probably this circumstance which first led him to forsake the cultivation of the opera for that of sacred music. At Düsseldorf he first designed his famous oratorio *St Paul*, in response to an application from the Cäcilien-Verein at Frankfort, composed his overture to *Die schöne Melusine*, and planned some other works of importance. He liked his appointment, and would probably have retained it much longer had he not been invited to undertake the permanent direction of the Gewandhaus concerts at Leipzig, and thus raised to the highest position attainable in the German musical world. To this new sphere of labour he removed in August 1835, opening the first concert at the Gewandhaus, on the 4th of October, with his overture *Die Meeresstille*, a work possessing great attractions, though by no means on a level with the *Midsummer Night's Dream*, *The Isles of Fingal*, or *Melusine*.

Mendelssohn's reception in Leipzig was most enthusiastic; and under their new director the Gewandhaus concerts prospered exceedingly. Meanwhile *St Paul* steadily progressed, and was first produced, with triumphant success, at the Lower Rhine festival at Düsseldorf, on the 22nd of May 1836. On the 3rd of October it was first sung in English, at Liverpool, under the direction of Sir George Smart; and on the 16th of March 1837 Mendelssohn again directed it at Leipzig.

The next great event in Mendelssohn's life was his happy marriage, on the 28th of March 1837, to Cecile Charlotte Sophie Jeanrenaud. The honeymoon was scarcely over before he was again summoned to England to conduct *St Paul*, at the Birmingham festival, on the 20th of September. During this visit he played on the organ at St Paul's and at Christ Church, Newgate Street, with an effect which exercised a lasting influence upon English organists. It was here also that he first contemplated the production of his second oratorio, *Elijah*.

Passing over the composition of the *Lobgesang* in 1840, a sixth visit to England in the same year, and his inauguration of a scheme for the erection of a monument to Sebastian Bach, we find Mendelssohn in 1841 recalled to Berlin by the king of Prussia, with the title of Kapellmeister. Though his appointment resulted in the production of *Antigone*, *Oedipus Coloneus*, *Athalie*, the incidental music to the *Midsummer Night's Dream*, and other great works, it proved an endless source of vexation, and certainly helped to shorten the composer's life. In 1842 he came to England for the seventh time, accompanied by his wife, conducted his Scotch symphony at the Philharmonic, again played the organ at St Peter's, Cornhill, and Christ Church, Newgate Street, and was received with honour by the queen and the prince consort. He did not, however, permit his new engagements to interfere with the direction of the Gewandhaus concerts; and in 1843 he founded in Leipzig the great conservatoire which soon became the best musical college in Europe, opening it on the 3rd of April in the buildings of the Gewandhaus. In 1844 he conducted six of the Philharmonic concerts in London, producing his new *Midsummer Night's Dream* music, and playing Beethoven's pianoforte concerto in G with extraordinary effect. He returned to his duties at Berlin in September, but succeeded in persuading the king to free him from his most onerous engagements.

After a brief residence in Frankfort, Mendelssohn returned to Leipzig in September 1845, resuming his old duties at the Gewandhaus, and teaching regularly in the conservatoire. Here he remained, with little interruption, during the winter — introducing his friend Jenny Lind, then at the height of her popularity, to the critical frequenters of the Gewandhaus, and steadily working at *Elijah*, the first performance of which he conducted at the Birmingham festival, on the 26th of August 1846. The reception of this great work was enthusiastic. Unhappily, the excitement attendant upon its production, added to the irritating effect of the worries at Berlin, made a serious inroad upon the composer's health. On his return to Leipzig he worked on as usual, but it was clear that his health was seriously impaired. In 1847 he visited England for the tenth and last time, to conduct four performances of Elijah at Exeter Hall, on the 16th, 23rd, 28th and 30th of April, one at Manchester on the 20th, and one at Birmingham on the 27th. But the exertion was beyond his strength. He witnessed Jenny Lind's first appearance at Her Majesty's Theatre, on the 4th of May, and left England on the 9th, little anticipating the trial that awaited him in the tidings of the sudden death of his sister Fanny, which reached him only a few days after his arrival in Frankfort. The loss of his mother in 1842 had shaken him much, but the suddenness with which this last intelligence was communicated broke him down. He fell to the ground insensible, and never fully recovered. In June he was so far himself again that he was able to travel, with his family, by short stages, to Interlaken, where he stayed for some time, illustrating the journey by a series of water-colour drawings, but making no attempt at composition for many weeks. He returned to Leipzig in September, bringing with him fragments of *Christus, Loreley*, and some other unfinished works, taking no part in the concerts, and living in privacy. On the 9th of October he called on Madame Frege, and asked her to sing his latest set of songs. She left the room for lights, and on her return found him in violent pain and almost insensible. He lingered for four weeks, and on the 4th of November he passed away, in the presence of his wife, his brother, and his three friends, Moscheles, Schleinitz, and Ferdinand David. A cross marks the site of his grave, in the Alte Dreifaltigkeits Kirchhof, at Berlin.

Mendelssohn's title to a place among the great composers of the century is incontestable. His style, though differing little in technical arrangement from that of his classical predecessors, is characterized by a vein of melody peculiarly his own, and easily distinguishable by those who have studied his works, not only from the genuine effusions of contemporary writers, but from the most successful of the servile imitations with which, even during his lifetime, the music-shops were deluged. In less judicious hands the rigid symmetry of his phrasing might, perhaps, have palled upon the ear; but under his skilful management it serves only to impart an additional charm to thoughts which derive their chief beauty from the evident spontaneity of their conception. In this, as in all other matters of a purely technical character, he regarded the accepted laws of art as the medium by which he might most certainly attain the ends dictated by the inspiration of his genius. Though caring nothing for rules, except as means for producing a good effect, he scarcely ever violated them, and was never weary of impressing their value upon the minds of his pupils. His method of counterpoint was modelled in close accordance with that practised by Sebastian Bach. This he used in combination with an elastic development of the sonata-form, similar to that engrafted by Beethoven upon the lines laid down by Haydn. The principles involved in this arrangement were strictly conservative; yet they enabled him, at the very outset of his career, to invent a new style no less original than that of Schubert or Weber, and no less remarkable as the embodiment of canons already consecrated by classical authority than as a special manifestation of individual genius. It is thus that Mendelssohn stands before us as at the same time a champion of conservatism and an apostle of progress; and it is chiefly by virtue of these two apparently incongruous though really compatible phases of his artistic character that his influence and example availed, for so many years, to hold in check the violence of reactionary opinion which injudicious partisanship afterwards fanned into revolutionary fury.

Concerning Mendelssohn's private character there have never been two opinions. As a man of the world he was more than ordinarily accomplished — brilliant in conversation, and in his lighter moments overflowing with sparkling humour and ready pleasantry, loyal and unselfish in the more serious business of life, and never weary of working for the general good. As a friend he was unvaryingly kind, sympathetic and true. His earnestness as a Christian needs no stronger testimony than that afforded by his own delineation of the character of St Paul; but it is not too much to say that his heart and life were pure as those of a little child.

A BIOGRAPHY FROM
1911 *Encyclopædia Britannica, Volume* 18

Fantasy on "The Last Rose of Summer"

Op.15

Mendelssohn
Fantasy on "The Last Rose of Summer"
Op. 15

Tempo I

Andante con moto

CPSIA information can be obtained
at www.ICGtesting.com
Printed in the USA
BVHW012041090922
646660BV00009B/685